NEW YORK REVIEW BOOKS

POETS

AMELIA ROSSELLI (1930–1996) was born in Paris to the Italian intellectual Carlo Rosselli and the English Quaker activist Marion Cave. After her father and uncle were assassinated by Fascists in 1937, Rosselli spent a peripatetic childhood in France, Switzerland, England, and the United States, returning to Italy at the end of World War II. In Rome, she became close with Alberto Moravia (her first cousin) and Pier Paolo Pasolini while working as a typist and translator of English for Adriano Olivetti's Edizioni di Comunità. Although she attended meetings of the avant-garde Gruppo 63, she tended to keep an ironic distance from their pronouncements. In addition to her accomplishments as a poet, Rosselli was a serious musician and student of musicology who collaborated with John Cage and David Tudor. Among her many books of poetry are *War Variations* (1964), *Hospital Series* (1969), and *Impromptu* (1981). Rosselli suffered from mental illness for much of her adult life and committed suicide at the age of sixty-five.

BARRY SCHWABSKY is the art critic for *The Nation* and co-editor of international reviews for *Artforum*. His recent books include *The Perpetual Guest: Art in the Unfinished Present* (2016) and *The Observer Effect: On Contemporary Painting* (2019) as well as two collections of poetry, *Feelings of And* (2022) and *Water from Another Source* (2023).

T0342001

Amelia Rosselli

Sleep

INTRODUCTION BY BARRY SCHWABSKY

NYRB/POETS

 NEW YORK REVIEW BOOKS   *New York*

THIS IS A NEW YORK REVIEW BOOK
PUBLISHED BY THE NEW YORK REVIEW OF BOOKS
207 East 32nd Street, New York, NY 10016
www.nyrb.com

Library of Congress Cataloging-in-Publication Data
  Names: Rosselli, Amelia, 1930–1996, author. | Schwabsky, Barry, writer of
  introduction.
Title: Sleep / by Amelia Rosselli ; introduction by Barry Schwabsky.
Description: New York : New York Review Books, [2023] | Series: New
  York Review Books poets
Identifiers: LCCN 2023017246 (print) | LCCN 2023017247 (ebook) | ISBN
  9781681377834 (paperback) | ISBN 9781681377841 (ebook)
Subjects: LCGFT: Poetry.
Classification: LCC PR9120.9.R67 S63 2023 (print) | LCC PR9120.9.R67
  (ebook) | DDC 811/.54—dc23/eng/20230516
LC record available at https://lccn.loc.gov/2023017246
LC ebook record available at https://lccn.loc.gov/2023017247

ISBN 978-1-68137-783-4
Available as an electronic book; ISBN 978-1-68137-784-1

Cover and book design by Emily Singer

Printed in the United States of America on acid-free paper.
10 9 8 7 6 5 4 3 2 1

Contents

THIS IS NOT QUITE the first publication for anglophone readers of Amelia Rosselli's poetry written in English, but almost. Six of the poems appeared in 1966 in *Art and Literature*, the now-legendary Swiss-based magazine edited by John Ashbery, Ann Dunn, Rodrigo Moynihan, and Sonia Orwell—the connection seems to have been through Ashbery, though when I asked him, not long before his death, how this had come about, he couldn't recall—and another in *The Times Literary Supplement*. After that they were unavailable anywhere until the 1980s, when Rosselli published a few in Italian journals alongside her own translations. Twenty of the poems were published as a small book in 1989 under the title *Sonno–Sleep (1953–1966)*, with Italian versions by Antonio Porta, another of the major Italian poets of Rosselli's generation. A fuller collection (eighty-eight poems) only appeared in 1992 as *Sleep: Poesie in inglese*, with a facing translation into Italian by the scholar Emmanuela Tandello. Most recently, *Sleep* was part of the 2012 collection *L'Opera poetica*, edited by Stefano Giovanuzzi (and with an introduction by Tandello) as a volume in the Meridiani series, the Italian equivalent of France's Pleiade—the first really complete presentation of the text, with the eighty-eight poems from the 1992 collections alongside thirty-eight "poems omitted from *Sleep*" (including two that were published with Porta's translations in the 1989 booklet). As for the omitted poems, it should not be imagined that they are inferior to those that were included. In making her selection, Rosselli seems primarily to have been concerned with the poems' translatability, telling Tandello that some were "beautiful in English and definitively bad if translated into Italian." At this distance it's hard to see how the poet made her division between the damned and the saved.

The poems in *Sleep* were written, according to Tandello, in three campaigns—1953–1955, 1960–1961, and 1965–1966—which is to say that they overlap with those of her first book in Italian, *Variazioni belliche*, dated 1959–1961 and published in 1964, as well as her second, *Serie ospedaliera*, dated 1958 and 1963–1965, published in 1969. The completion of the project links up with the start of work on *Documento* (1966–1973), a book—as she wrote to her brother John in England in 1970—"which at the moment I hope will be my last," and which came out in 1976. (In fact Rosselli had, along with some retrospective gatherings of earlier work, one more new book in her, the aptly titled *Impromptu*, written suddenly in 1979, after six years of silence, and published two years later.)

Although Rosselli's most productive period encompassed the mid-1950s through the early 1970s, her Italian poetry only started to become accessible to readers of English in 2003, when Lucia Re and Paul Vangelisti published their version of her first book, *War Variations*. Many more translations have appeared since then, but her English-language writing has remained unavailable. How did it happen that an Italian poet composed such an extensive body of work in English? One answer starts from the fact that it was never fated that Italian would be her primary language. Rosselli was born in 1930 in Paris. Her father, Carlo, the scion of a prominent Italian Jewish family, was a leading anti-Fascist activist living in exile; her mother, Marion Cave, was an English Quaker. After Carlo's assassination at Mussolini's behest in 1937, the family moved to England, then Switzerland, and finally Larchmont, New York, where she attended Mamaroneck High School. Rosselli visited Italy for the first time in 1946, but soon found herself in London as a student at the prestigious St. Paul's Girls' School, where her interest in music flourished. Only at the end of 1949 did Rosselli return definitively to Italy; she did not obtain permanent residency there until 1959. Italy was a determinate choice on her part, not a default—and the same goes for the Italian language. But that means there were other choices open to her.

In Rome, Rosselli soon met the poet Rocco Scotellaro, seven years older, an event she considered "fundamental": "It was through him that I discovered the Italian poets and learned to write verse in Italian. Not that I didn't know Italian, I'd never thought of becoming a poet." But in the mid-1950s, she was writing not only in Italian but in French and English. In 1980 she would publish the collection *Primi Scritti (1952–1963)*, which she considered "the kind of book that's published posthumously." It comprises, alongside writing in Italian and French, two prose pieces in English as well as a cycle of poems, "October Elizabethans," that exaggerate to a ludicrous degree the parodic antiquarianism found in more homeopathic doses throughout *Sleep*. *Primi Scritti* also includes a formerly fractured "Diario in Tre Lingue," one of whose last lines is "Let's see if we can sleep now..." Finally, it should be noted that, aside from *Sleep* and the work in *Primi Scritti*, Rosselli's oeuvre includes two more brief poems in English, both unpublished in her lifetime. One is dated 1995; the other was found inscribed in her copy of the poems of Emily Dickinson—the book itself is marked "Rosselli '65," presumably the date it was purchased or read; but I wonder if the poem itself does not also date from the mid-1990s, when Rosselli was asked to translate ten of Dickinson's poems for the Meridiani edition of the American's work, which appeared in 1997, the year after Rosselli's death by suicide.

Given her partly American upbringing, not to mention having a British mother, Rosselli did not encounter English as a foreigner, and yet the language of *Sleep* is hardly the vernacular with which we are familiar. Just as Rosselli's Italian poetry incorporates dissonantly non-Italian elements, as if she were translating on the fly from her linguistically multiple imagination, her English-language poetry accommodates phrasing that may not quite feel like English. And it's full of strange and unpredictable shifts between contemporary and obsolete usage, both British and American; odd neologisms ("benixt," "homicile"), archaisms ("shallops," "sipid") and un- or eccentric grammaticalities ("pansies" as a verb, "hoped" or "inflationed" as adjectives), all used strikingly but sparingly. So when she writes, "we call out help! /

and fall drit / into a mire which is our belonging," that pe-culiar "drit" is somehow both the Middle English word for excrement, which developed into our modern word "dirt," but also the Italian "*dritti*"—straight. The poems are stud-ded with internal rhymes—never end rhymes—that seem to fracture the lines in which they occur even as they create contrapuntal linkages from line to line: an exacerbated form of enjambement, perhaps. Diction and sometimes spellings are borrowed freely from the poetry of the seventeenth cen-tury—most notably John Donne and, of course, Shakespeare: the book's very title evokes Hamlet's soliloquy. Rosselli came of age as a poet at a time when T. S. Eliot's polemic in favor of the Metaphysical poets as "the direct current of Eng-lish poetry," showing the modernist how to be "more com-prehensive, more allusive, more indirect, in order to force, to dislocate if necessary, language into his meaning," was at its most powerful. If the result of Eliot's influence on postwar American poetry was not entirely happy—one recalls Wil-liam Carlos Williams's lament that "Eliot returned us to the classroom just at the moment when I felt we were on a point to escape to matters much closer to the essence of a new art form"—Rosselli's assimilation of Metaphysical dislocation via parody and pastiche never had a chance of settling into an orthodoxy. In any case, the fraught divisions of the Anglo-American poetry world were irrelevant to her, and she was equally attentive to Charles Olson and John Berryman. Among Rosselli's American contemporaries, the most im-portant to her may have been Sylvia Plath, whose poetry she translated into Italian. In an interview, Rosselli explained that what interested her in Plath was "her musicality, certain technical procedures, stylistic inversions," rather than the personal tenor of her subject matter. "I see something of myself, too," Rosselli continued, "in her sense of color, in a religious feeling that's sometimes restrained but other times bursts forth uncontrollably, in a linguistic breadth that's anything but academic. The writer is a person entirely alone, spiritually, stylistically alone."

Rosselli's is as unique a voice in English, as stylistically alone, as she is in what Lucia Re has called her "'disturbed' yet highly controlled Italian." In either language, what counts is that, as she once explained, "poetic form has for me been connected to its more strictly musical sense, and in truth I've never observed a distinction between the two disciplines, considering the syllable not just as an orthographic nexus but as a sound, and the sentence not only as a grammatical construct but as a system"—though she was quick to clarify that this *sound* that is the spoken syllable should more properly be considered a *noise*. Rosselli's music of linguistic noises is strictly measured. The passionate violence of her language is rational, her expressive extremism steeped in formality. An ironic self-consciousness is ever-present, yet the result is not an equilibrium or resolution but a scathing counterattack—in *Sleep*, against an unnamed "he" who seems to stand in for all the male speakers who in the poetic tradition complain so bitterly about their treatment by the female love object. The tables are turned and the man becomes the silent listener to the litany of his wrongs. Neither lover is individuated; any one could stand for all. This is a poetry in which it can happen that "radioactive confusion bit into my / brain radiant with multitudes." Unlike most of the Americans influenced by Eliot's encomium of the Metaphysicals, Rosselli did not forget his admonition that the poet looks not only into the heart but "into the cerebral cortex, the nervous system, and the digestive tracts." While too many stopped at the cerebrum, Rosselli's poetry is steeped in corporeal experience. Thus unhappy lovers:

> Their bones
> grew to them huge, an apparel
> heavy to handle. As if in the
> fit of love their digestions
> troubled them.

How will *Sleep* be digested, or trouble the digestion, as anglophone readers finally begin to come to terms with it? It won't be easy, because Rosselli's distinctive approach to poetic form is hardly comparable to that of any of her American or British contemporaries. And yet in her fierce and anarchic irony, her inverted and *détourned* formality, we recognize a kinship with a constellation of Anglo-American voices, from precursors like Mina Loy to certain British poets of the 1970s, such as Veronica Forrest-Thomson or Anna Mendelssohn, and contemporary Americans, including Joyelle McSweeney and Catherine Wagner, all of whom confront us with questions like Rosselli's "Who am I talking to? Who asks me / anything? What rebel use have you / for my jargon?" And if we can learn to read Loy and the rest, we can learn to read Rosselli too.

—*Barry Schwabsky*

Sleep

What woke those tender heavy fat hands
said the executioner as the hatchet fell
down upon their bodily stripped souls
fermenting in the dust. You are a stranger here
and have no place among us. We would have you off our list
of potent able men
were it not that you've never belonged to it. Smell
the cool sweet fragrance of the incense burnt, in honour
of some secret soul gone off to enjoy an hour's agony
with our saintly Maker. Pray be away
sang the hatchet as it cut slittingly
purpled with blood. The earth is made nearly
round, and fuel is burnt every day of our lives.

hell, loomed out
with perfect hands.

Well, so, patience to our souls
the seas run cold, 'pon our bare necks
shivered. We shall eat out of our bare hand
smiling vainly. The silver pot is snapped;
we be snapped out of boredom, in a jiffy-
run. Tentacles of passion run rose-wise
like flaming strands of opaque red lava. Our soul
tears with passion, its chimney. The wind cries oof!
and goes off. We were left alone with our sister
navel. Good, so we'll learn to
ravish it. Alone. Words in their forge.

the cherry bee stands on the apple tree
in full bloom; i cut a road to hell
with my own footling. Drones the humming-bee;
it never sought God, nor found it.

the leaves are crushing the wind

                    gone my love negates
disremembers. Otello has taken
the wheel in hand, his
broken fingers icily clasp
the silver pumice. O land of Sicily my heart
is sick with hoping, mows
the tavern its clanging bell
rust-fouled, and the grey
cloak of love tenderly
dies anew.

                    at the corner the dew
on the corpse awaits stiff
unaware of the many purposeless
strings it holds in its hand. Awaits
a greater danger yet a greater
shiver in the dusk slips the sleeper
down the foaming steps of hell and the garage
holds wide
its hoary cavern mouth.

Ye who do Batter me with Wordes
be Still: my Soul does rise in Silence
up the Sordid Moon

so finally we have reached the level our self had
meant reach, about a month ago, planning
rack into the future Ω sing we, with one
short glance into the
arabic grammar, sing we, then
'(i say), sing we uplifted from the
ground and as yet not
quite at the heavens, but static
in our own innumerable undescribable
tension of love fear and all that god
has replenished the world with, time merrily
chirping at the great wide interlaced gates
opening finally at our demonish
will but now is it god's!

upon the hearing of certain dissonances in the slow moonlight

as that which frozen neither of us understands
is out and above our hopes, perhaps that
is true love, said the bag-pipe as it
froze out. As slowly with circumvolution the notes spake out
i shut my eyes and sang slowly, slight nip
into the beat of all multitudes.

the rose and the dew
are but images of you; little
symbols, upon the great rack. O
rack, rack, 'tis then he sat
in full quid. The rose said: phew!,
but the dew answered not (kept a reserved
demeanour), and so all finished in the
Jack Pot, afatigued from night watches.

o the trees are wild with winter tension
and the leaves rush upon the big mat
gallop-horsed
(and the leaves tumble like wild birds on the heath)

the terrible transport of love
(a hidden fibre of
hate) recovers its
grace, when we slip
by its roaring gate. Do
come rose
dew
kill the cold horse
galloping its mane flying outwards

o the shallops put out to sea and we remain ashore
gnawing into the salt bread of
disaster (his is a used
phrase, and we do
prefer it).

Ashore's the great servility
mobile on its two-legged carts
stripped-eased
by the road. A soldier wooden he
staked by the running homicile
flash-deep. Out your cross
out the bloody banner
and we shall fall stop. Oh the guards
do catch with us:
then hard-pressed time
cracks
rut.

I hear the wind whisper my ears
his great stock of travails
I hear the wind continue
travail. I hear fortune bending its
arrow-back, and the
wind
arch its back.

you seem to hear angels mocking you,
you seem to cry out look the stars!
and run out rapid against a fence of spine.

no i did not love you i see this clear again or think i do
find my heart fundamentally cold yet
it was before a stone of heat, begging
to aid you come to the final point
between us, and so again i part from you and
never must i seek again to find you helpless
in my grasp, never more shall i put the
ax between us never shall i run to you crying
see this music!

                              Time
drags and breaks. O, come and deliver me
from the wooden frog! (Anaverta inadvertently
spreads out her fan.)
    Yes Canada, o Canada
to *you* I refer.

those thoughts which most appealingly had made me closer
to your being
must be flung off, lest i die.
o is it life we nevertheless do but keep
off, curiously warm,
or does then god play skillfully with me, that nevermore i
should meet you at the point where all desire
dies, and joy alone
rule
the brazen cars.

never had i searched for
this calm has assailed me, never had i thought
to rest again in the soft moss of
joy furthermore never had i suspected
calm might rise from the acrid delirium which
had ruled me sick upon the loop
of indecision. weakness you have been my master
and my ruler yet you have brought me to the place where
                                                    [slow
love and calm decision best do their
trick, work upon the loom secretly with my full
assent. do not question now you have
found what you have got however you have
received it yet i know the strange
illumination at the end of endless
walks waisted upon the heel of
tautness have brought me lived again into the
sun warm into its own darkness. silver knot of choice i
have followed you without a doubt you were
work of the devil yet you have brought me
reeling into god the moon and the stars and
no road clearer lead before to such
chance but by chance, the very devil's chance followed
congruously without a hope of gain save that of
saving the face of the devil without one least
sob. so god i must recognize you were the work of the
devil which i followed with
hidden heart and no thought whatever save that
of saving what rested of hatred and impatience
turmoil in my blood and the thought of god
hidden in the folds of all impatience.

a soft sonnet is all the strength i have
to create, full easy life have i ever and ever
again and again destroyed, but was it god crying
within me turn out all
lights! No love be granted to he who
hates all love save life
writ on paper there goes my
seed wild into
death.

ha so you had thought you would have found felicity
at the corner drug-
store, and are once more deluded, o you who wait
timelessly at the fountain and are shoved
back into your own
lair. nevermore nevermore do we say upon
each division from
glory, nevermore shall we illude our senses our very
essence, that again the blood might run fresh upon the white
block. Bring in your heavy load of dry herbs bring
in your pain and keep it frozen to your own
essence, it might shind itself into
white light, if you but
dig into it.

we have newly learned to sin, to sing that
is, with the hatchet behind our
shoulders but nevertheless we
sing
wildly
before god discovers our disgrace, quick
hidden in the wings of all
falsehood, joy is an everlasting
sorrow.

a hundred times must i flow o'er the tiger trees
that the pomegranates may burst. O leprosy
that has assailed me, the wind sings purple
to my bent ears, the seas turn purple
to my blind eyes, and i sing (i sink) into
night's black prayer, softer than all the trees all the skies
                                        [all the seas.

the lovely train of thought
which had closest brought me farthest from
your
tight closet, returns, shivering
with the lighted beacon of a distressed
permit of pain. The lighted beacon which had
furthest announced its rainbow
joy, is delirious, soulfully
singing rot
into the crashed ears.

Long before the summer had flown, green grass
rotted on the ground: – long before my heart and
yours had played out, the green grass came to
sprout again. Long before the metre of our love
had fixed itself, my heart had given out, and
the sun still shone liquid and staring at my
tired eyes. Long before you had ever played with
chance, chance had begotten you. Then were we
all mute. Long before we had rested in iniquity
chance had played its part.

And then she left the convent (the interminable sick-
bed). Then she left charity! Then she found hope.
Then she left.

We drag on, earth bound, in our enchanting
spheres of half-knowledge, bewildered even
as love laughs through the clouds, I in
particular embarassment sat in the railway
car, half in hell. Earth bound as is our
severe training to human love, we love
no thing on earth, chanted train wheels
violently, as our hearts sank into balloons
of half-pity, half-love, hell's knowledge
of children, gaming with the keep that
kills them.

Hell, loomed out with perfect hands, wrapped
our glare with a fierce shudder of fright into
the night exchanged for a pair of rubies. Fright
Desdemona's petticure, was all-afrantic he
might come off rushing on the last bus, but
we were ready to admire his creative genius
and let nothing disturb us save the chime at
the door-bell when it rang off at its best.
Necessarily our gun-drop dropped off at hell's
timing: loomed out again into a wrapped parcel
containing all of our bodily food. Soul discomposed
watched from afar but no regard of angels enwrapped
his studious regard with love.

In the pale bloom of flower love laid hold of its
impossibility and swam back into the round shaped
earth waving tears of departure into the mist

The King and Queen sat beheaded firmly
embraced, enlaced in a fit of action troublesome
to their fitsome senses. A fire to my dandy
lover! responded the Queen to her lover's
embraces, a fire to the wine which scurries
in the veins of my beheaded head! The King
sat a-mused while he played with her hand,
dripping with the juice of his head. Her
head lay despondently on the rim of the
throne fit for a King to sit on, lest he
lose his Grace on the matrimonial day which
was granted by the Divinity on her losing
her socket which joined the bones of man
and women as they sat firmly embraced under
the pine-tree a-pining for the tree of love
soul-less as an apple. Joined by the knitted
brow of God, the Queen embraced her Courtly
lover and enlaced his firm pocket with gold
handkerchiefs with which to pine on. Weeping
for her primordial sin she whipped a bite
off the old pine-tree, and fell a-nursing
her teeth, troublesome to her mannered
head a-squinting in the foam of her death
grinned smile of a face, courtly notwithstanding
all. All sat and smiled and there was the
end of the travail she had undergone to
save her Master's soul under the pine-wood
tree of action.

In a fit they embraced, their destinies
close-linked to their pressing bones.

As if in a fit they did desist
from making love. Their bones
grew to them huge, an apparel
heavy to handle. As if in the
fit of love their digestions
troubled them. O love that entire
devotes its time to solitude!
Again we muse thy fate over
the childish brute of a world
tending
to mishap.

As if in a fit they did desist from loving
a true nest in the bare bread of love.
Again the farce lit the play and the actors
filed out over and above the stage: anon
it had been dark; it is light now, that
we two do not respond to our calling.

Love itself does shake off responsibilities
but for a time.

We had lit the world with our calling but
the ever-changing scenes at our window
of our souls cut by three giant trees sword
shaped drew from us heavy sighs.

It is your love has shaped me thus! exclaimed
the first damsel to her partner: no, it
is yours that has embittered the farce to
this sore point, declaimed the giant warrior.

I am in love with thee but for the farce!
exclaimed the giant pea drooping its flower
daintily over the moist earth. It is your
calling has developed the world, said love
again to its children, who browsed over
books, rooks and channels seeking the entrance
out. Of mishap we know but the name, yet
our gentle brook, rook-called, (the giant
trees unfurl their tender light by the night
light of a waning moon) the giant trees
do but unfurl the development of our love,
the brook chants to the rook: – black raven
collapsing into the science of every-day
transport. We are at ease here by the brook,
evanescent as the sun at its setting. As

the earth drew its moist sigh, a tear fell
to the ground upon the enclasped hands of
the twin lovers. The winds, pushed by their
twin breaths, developed a current of air

sighing into the clouds.

To call to love is but to make the name
of usury! This ever-precious stone on your

neck droops too far out of my reach and
your tender hands clasping the broom of

severity do but cut a slice into the heart
of the matter which I hold in my own trembling

fingers.

All of God's yeomen were cowards!
All of God's men were yeomen.

Webern Opus 4

military melancholy reverberates softly
on slender walls, as the sipid music rapidly
counterbounces against walls thicker than
can permit the rapid brain. Cultivation
of flowers is a soft pose in a bent garden
the gallant fingers reaching into crooked
petals are as if placing against an even
beat slow triolets.

impertinent with tears and impotent
with grief the heart attacks billowing
clouds tremendous on the outline
of the world gone. Sententious poetry
reclaims the fear in the grief while
tears sweep through the street. Impertinent
with grief and grieved with salt tears
awash on the balcony the youth sat
on his chair enjoyed the sun employed
his grief. Hasard being the king
of grief felicity swept the clouds
off.

slightly nauseated with all cry I fell
into bemused play, because God was not
in my face Since the cry had fallen
from the lips of the child my sleep had been
betroubled with cry, o soft shadow of sin you swamp
my heart's play.

radioactive confusion bit into my
brain radiant with multitudes. Unexpectedly
the lights warm in a heart went out
for the pleasure of separation. Encountering
the bell flashing in the eyes of
the partisan of a good cause, I
collapsed into fits of apology:
bragging into the tear-rid apostrophes
of saints.

Belonging to a race of saints the
upshot of this long separation which
we ourselves must set to our pleasures
the wind entered the broken boned
part of the heart freezing in a winter
grip.

Assertion of individuality broke
up the cupid love he held for senseless
mates of joy. Regardless of impossibility
the fire turned over the spittled
chicken, as it twisted plumed. Against
triviality the spit hung a banner
pierced through your heart encountered
flames of lust. Through the key hole
of an old woman's bed room door appeared
to the distraught eye the weight
of all disaster.

The soft agate eye of the neighbor had transfixed
my imagination, which bent into ulterior
motives such as weariness and the best attirement
for some kind pain which would forever guarantee
another life. The other life however displayed
a rather forgetful costume, simpering against
the heavy rain turning into a marasmus my
forgetful heart, now reminded of its own
weariness as the car drove through the blank
hills.

Sleep

slightly nauseated with all cry I fell
into bemused sleep, oh the tender dangerous
virgins on the mountain top watch a sleep
which is not mine since the radiant bed
of earth covered me moss like. I am a
broken fellow cried the fish monger, and
belayed his true nature. I am the bemused
man on the tree top cried the arch duke
pleased he had slept with divinity. I am
the cry in the night exclaimed the author
as his book fell. The sun slept into a
douche of cloud like sun drop, the earth
rounded the point. All cry is a massacre
when sleep is the virgin; the reason is
lost when all impatience is neglected.

The banality of all superiors is a danger
for the host. The intricacies of court
life is the danger. I am the danger of
a court massacre, exclaimed the virgin
on the tree top as the tree fell, swarmed
down to putritude. Sleep fell on, the reason
went, and the host remembered he had forgotten
the power and the glory.

The hard eyes of the lucky few were a benediction to the lower multitude. Perhaps you have mislaid my heart, she thought as he climbed upon her, thank less of a smile. Benixt the shoes that stamp on her heart is the iced river which flows beneath your soul. A rough river divided their hearts and a monster, hard eyed, begot them and betrayed them.

Summoned by the police she ran home left the party of the brawling few. Bring your purse with you cried her guardian nevertheless another chance begot her too.

Worthless as was her itinerary to fame
she collapsed unexpectedly into a mirrored
frame which was the sordid history of
the resistance of the few to the world's
massacre. Collapse into my brother's arms,
shiver down my faultless spine of woe! Thus
a weary maiden quivered slight into arms
softer than her brother's arms, her forces,
slippery as a horse's cry, her quivered
hopes of gain collapsed suddenly into a fresh
bargain unutterable.

1)

Ravish the import of cigarettes when they monstrously
decide you'd better stop. When the decline and fall
of even march supported better than I the ascent of
deliverance, we sat still. Momentaneous the silence
a moment ago you spoke.
                              Still and forever you spoke
against the livery of a blue sky, tyranny of images
here you come again. Preparing the downfall of strips
of teasing talk was the grey upshot of the conversation
which in cannibal laughter demonstrated its impreparation.
When the thought of the winter brought us too close
to winter tension we spoke, of bravery and the horses
revelling in dust and blood turmoiled. Prepare your
life to the hidden atmosphere which betrays, sit still
in the uproar of events, turmoil in your blood better
hides ferocity.
                    When in the street rang the bells of Sunday we
spoke and laughed, left off waiting, and forever attending
the revolution of the heart, we spoke again: free
intermission of the soul while beckons order.

In the order of the straight streets beckons my orderly
upturning of life: be gone, you who disrupt the rigour
of void and the scarlet letter written to my soul
an agony in waiting.

Streets disrupted again the straight heart cannot
withstand the turn of life, be gone, says he to the
chaos which beckons.

2)

No solution to your feeling to your thinking of
everything a pearl of choice of damnation in the
white streets of Sunday. The post, long prepared
by the barrel, waits: you must go, throw the letter
down the steps which declaim events, decisions,
foam at your mouth proclaims disquisitions. Decide
against every even spent understanding that three
are the scales: preparation morality and turpitude.
When the descent to the foaming steps revealed
unnecessary error you were ready to exchange all
your land for deity.

But I do not see the answer! long prepared diagnosis
of the brave you have left me astrand. When the
winter callus on my feet proclaimed originality
we left off searching and referred to science of
curiosity, boredom under a new hat, the white marmalade
of choices left to chance, if periodically you
must lose and find yourself but for a pause. Oh
pause then my heart in search of livery, pause
your breath on these twin steps: the history, the
failure and the bitter joy of blind friendship.

We saw the king: we bowed, turned our backs hesitantly
but finding no approval, swam back home: to the
new morality: a squirt at chance, a spirit forlorn
when the sky at its most purple point trebled the
irradiation of love.

Straight as a shaft of light she fled from
the cunning race, fled into the hangar, black
almost since its grey was clear. And in the straights
of these definite standings she understood perhaps
to have beloved all the world with too much
intensity, and herself, the queen of it, as it
ran ramshackle into the hangar, a plane on its
way to triumph or its own perdition.

The hangar closed down: bent on practicability.
She returned head lowered and a bordered belt
on the sides, a trifle blowsy, but perhaps moderate
enough in her judgement, to an old apprehension
or acceptance of the causes: lower your nets
when the fish drag, and clear the decks from
all damaging surf! A plane, then a ship, all
moderate means, and her belted waist in accordance
with these laws of speed.

Must I tire my mind out
with absurd tyrannies, when
obviously the seaside roars
to tell far better stories
in a crash of lovingness?
Must I walk the plain or
the sea shore, with such
uncanny unreasoning, as
is yet mine? Must I wait,
stand, pray, and not answer
any of the bells tolling
pleasantly out to sea? When
the foremost bell rang sharp
out again or thrice she
drove the elephant by its
white tail to the sea shore
and had it grasp the single
utter meaning of the spell
the sea could cast.

a shaft of white light
on the featherdown
and all the pink
which falls beneath
its dust and shudder

the shutters failing
below, and the narrow
stairs, curving
too low.

Commemorating this year's
pink places, found
again
under the pear tree.

three-surfaced corner
up above
the angle beholding
my alcove

and sinewed strength
far-reaching
resolving to soar
by breaching
all the laws on board.

Aged man
on the corner
your mouth twists
out of order

and the mellow beach
near here
is out of reach
of your leer.

too vast a promontory for my sight
is this hill of belief: too vast
a thought you hide from my sight
this hill which slopes.

too strange a coincidence, your hand
on mine.

We are three
in our tree
eating, if
permissible
skies, and
flies, or
battles roving
in our eyes.

you might as well think one thing or another
of me; I am not at mercy's chance, nor do
I want your interpretation, having none
myself to overpower me. You withdraw into
your fevered cell, like a microscopic angel
do engage battle with my thoughts, as if
they were to my revolutionary heart, a
promiscuous bell. Hell itself is what you
want: a needle into necessity, foreseeing
I shall not do better than you want.

Actions in my brain: these verbs, whose celerity
resists all pain. Tenderness itself is dangerous
when out of claim; quick birds these verbs
do claim ignorance. The black branch of thought
leaves no life to thought; it resists all
cankering with craft, spice, tiresome desires
and tries, in its black fashion that it should
not die.

Spices too dull for any brain refrain from
tinkering with the business: a solace to
warm limbs.

Negro blood flowing on his brown
or black body, grace and length enticing
looks of envy, looks of rapture
records of tolerance.

Swimming underwater he saw all
life deformed; a virgin pen wrote
his name down.

If my mind were fit a king's, it would survey
all matters of the matter in a grey cloak, surrounding
its body with mist. But it does not shake off
thoughts which farces blur, it does not shake
off the light which dingy stamps pansies on its
rear – it only warns and fears – save me, from
my troublesome toil.

And its gears screech up to a screeching stop,
a sudden understanding or understatement: it
defies no right for it to sit proper in the rear
but that you allow it. You will have no purpose
from it save that it cannot afford to waste such
time and weight as you propose. It affords no
somnolence but that you have won the party. It
allows all geese loose in its dormitory, till
they light up in a flight of images. And then
sits still, taking calmly the drug of best behaviour
from your tawny hands which persevere in calling
it reversible, without claim, till it hangs,
suffocated, as if in a cellar were not best wine.

If you take a sip at it it will die, beset by
insomnia, long-lived girlhood peeking at night.
If it will hang hang it with all your might to
some tree whose weight will bear the might, which
turned loose revealed itself without a crêpe
save that you touched it.

Do come see my poetry
sit for a portrait, it
hangs in dimples, by the
light bay window, and pronounces
no shape of word, but that
you find it imperative.

Do come see me writhe, in
the shadows of lust, as
if the sun had cleared
it from all narrow doubt.

Do see it shake off all
posts with a stick, hitting
the air, in long shadows.
It never made better claim
before, than to turn you
loose upon my sorrows.

hangs clatter round the head
as if transparency itself believed
to be but small bulwark to its
mission: cutting straight into
the heart.

hangs clatter on the bough, as
if all despondency came from
within, and sunshine were a ray
of freedom exorbitant of your
body. Hangs clatter on the spot
you choose to frequent, sore
point in the general plan of
things, cutting risks out of
matter.

hangs noise, sound, matter, all
sorts of things round your sprig
of a body – it withstands all,
turning to its own turnpike.
Hangs water in your mouth to
signify you may mellow, all things
within, outdoors, in the tremulous
wave of the hand.

Wash arms, legs, then your whole body
in stupefaction as to its cleanliness, then
bow down to evidence, and display an
evident need of distraction.

Jumping on the road you follow up, time and
again, the urge to disenchant, your
powers, then think it over once more step
out of reach.

Slipping out the paradox at its poignant
moment, then filling it up again, at the
proposal, that you open a score, of good
will and bad will.

But if you choose to store, all by yourself
knowledge against others, no good shall befall
your stock of novels. (While time and again
nods the beast of providence)

Then you got reality: at the age of thirty-three
dying on the cross, at cross-country, murdering
your parents' parents, saying that which was true
to your cumbersome nature. Then you got a sort
of freedom, by playing truant to all good causes
then you fetched the seamstress, and she put things
straight. Then you found hope, hung high up on
the tree, graspable, but too weighty a pride for
you to have a touch upon. Then tell me what you
found: a shilling, for your life's worth.

The children were scrambling by the nearby road
reaching a steady level, then letting loose. They
talked all night, of things pathetic, cumbersome,
pathological, sordid, pornographic, at last spiritual
as if the forces you let loose were preface to
preface. They found you'd not lost the host or
the power: only the life, which had lasted too
long. Then they set aside even pride, and banged
upon their hammers to remind you their truth: no
tragedies in their living, save that it may be
surmised. Setting aside all pride their hearts
gave bent to long sighs which showing upon the
surface of the moon, reflected strong eyes, ties
balloons of ability. In the void of mortal power
all change must take a turn: kill you down and
suffer you be the host.

Do come see my poetry
demand it sit for a portrait
in silence recalling
all past experiences
with no boredom enslaving
its cheeks which wait.

Do come see my poetry
be forceful and desperate
(if ever desperation were ever
a nest in the mind). In kind
it is suave almost, but rather
uncertain as to its premises
and as to its finalities
it avoids gaps, principles,
rests on unconscious decision
while you paint.

With a stroke of the brush you
empower it, with a bliss which
was not there, before we talked.
With a slip of the pen you
endow it, with thoughts which
were never there at all, save
that you lurked in the shadows
finding out its message.

And now the sitting is at end
your new principle stares
you in the eyes, and with dread
it surmises, you were never
born before you wrote
of tender surmises.

The marshes came to an end. We strove on a-glittering
with hoped fuel. The light shone strong
on limbs too weak to protest. Fire is the
light in my dandy's eye, while he strives
on to attitudes.

Right in the middle of the eye, swung a
battle, too hopeful to be lost. Right on
the right side of things, swung a hope,
too weak to be admitted. She sloped conveniences
into a shaft of righteousness, till it

admitted defeat.

We are three; handicapped by life nevertheless
fiercely ready for action; yet; with our
souls; with our hands and our shoes; we
learn there is no rivalry; we know we
see there is hope for a strong new tie
ready for delivery.

We are ready yes! we are here, yes! The
no of negation is being swept away, we
do exist, half out of way of chance.

A row was made at this declaration, a healthy
sort of impossibility had set us free, of
decadence. The zero hour had come: a black
funeral, a healthy resort; its three-pointed
hat belligerent with fame.

Death, death again do come, rise up again
you ghost of paradise, its celerity seems
to partake of greed; yet, why? yes, its
purple attitude defies even love.

Which crowned with thorns itself had dared
be the round point of center, of hope; which
blue with greed had decidedly turned against
manipulation of the material at hand; its
hand scratching into the dust of rivalry
or bark grabbing at the mystery.

We pointed inflationed hands towards a
new dark grey purple spot: its lunacy, that
it should so swear at liveliness. Withheld
from fame, turning to marshes, holding
back its pistol, grabbing the air with
its unwithheld hand: it swore; never to
parley with angels, nevermore: but bring
the spirit up turmoiling lovingly into
the rest of the place: a point in space
a sharp whistle, and two doors standing
ajar, clapping down the thunder, aggravating
desire of death.

you sweet, sweet, sweet, child, onwards, you
delicate overhauled train turning into pale
crimson detail; you belligerent waste, you
penetrating delicacy, you saliva watching
into the mystery of death which is a penetration
overhauling its entries, the way out is paved
with bad intentions, I summarize, that you
could not know he that made you. He is gentile
in his fashion and descending tent-wise to
the general hospitals; he is a tender fright
and a refrigerator; he is myself even, though
obtenebrated by joy.

You self-taught heart who has understood
its weak point, obduring through winters
too great for harmony. You tent of oxygen
you pale brown orange-leaved overhauling
though with your pen you may think, and analyse
encounters or things into being, they escape
you not without poverty, they take your hand
and beg: express me!

Who am I talking to? Who asks me
anything? What rebel use have you
for my jargon? Why cry, why stamp
your feet on this hot ground, rain
ridden, of the tears which fall beloving
on your hot head.

Why stamp your feet? Why cry in
fragile night, if angels watch and
stamp their feet, on the bottom
of your heart, fragile and forgiving?
Oh my hot soul: they, the rich, in
mind and matter, would quiet you
would prefer you keep safe out of
the way of eventual murder.

In the ways of the rich (their poor
jargon) lies this brilliant thirst:
to forgive you, and pass on then
to thirsty revenge, if you will
but allow me to even shake your
tips, your cold and warm hands, clasping.

Since you tried out in many myriad
shaped angles this thirst for anger,
this your murder: you gave in: be
poor, do not mismanage things flowing
along your red roots.

(He sits and cries but won't give
in to solace, the mother of the
prince, as he rolled along, slumbering
on warm cushions: your gift, your
promenade, your bearing with me,
along with all red roots).

Pardon in the shape of mother with
her pale pink lipstick sticks out
its tongue at me: you do not follow
it, the prince who sits, eating jam.
She overrules your bread-hot band
of pearls round the brain, will
not give in to princely pride, or
its hot intershade: your jam.

She overrules? She bends your pride;
the warm lisping barrel, the cavalry
rushing, are all but princely gifts
towards sheep, grazing in the grass
their bended eyes follow you hence.

And yet a lamb insists he be remembered:
grow your beard, put on whiskers,
you'll never have me out of your
hand. (And thrice she shifted rule
into comfort; beast into play, browsing
contemporaneously with the great
but feeling the field, lisping the
three-hatched gum-stuck hole of
a home: your teats, your mother-
attitude, your smallest worms, giants
in the passion.)

Do I want to participate, or don't
I want to participate in this black
hell of a road, its trees gently
begging for caress. Am I this passive
flower curving for wood and salt
to ground pestering its strings
of roots: or am I blood-thirsty
for cringing for propriety. Will
your self be home made, or simply
will you laugh at your attitudes
and stray astrand, gunpowdering
your mouth. I am not he I cry and
sing a song of beatitude, quite
unafraid you might come hammer me.

Am I a turnip? a string of pearls
or the safe ground on which to bear
weights?

Which unloading themselves filled
the roaring road with decency, surveillance
of this year's hopes: ill made, I
rather rest, than hear your wail
and string your pearls.

they scrabble: hiss and fear and belittle
every twitch of your nerves: serving higher
ideals as if it were a soup: to be fried
in, or held astance with light grip. They
swallow the meat in the jargon as if it
were a pauper's den, this hell (the naked
word) (or world).

They multiply your reflexes, enjoy your
causing them trouble and their firm (not
so very firm) grasp is a hold on your imagination
which crouching, affirms: you're not my
sorry king; it's gone, that king, he's gone
that shaft of marmalade lightning, the hiss
in the prayer.

And bent to ground your hips devout verify
there is no lightning, but only more soup
more meat, more fast – the choice of which
is almost left to chance.

She sits and waits and learns her fate
laughing away clouds, drooping over the
hangings tenderly; she sits and sleeps
away difficulties, marauding in her heart
which as a belly jarred to full stop unless
the beer be poured out juicily.

She waits and bears the weight of an electric
lightning swinging in the poor troublesome
semi-tired heart of her apparel: a juice
poured out fully: her even chance, to
scorn fellow men.

Follow me, follow me! she cries and wipes
distances from her eyes. Pride never swung
so long as to prefer strong strength to
my bow tie exclaimed she ringingly: you
fear the night, you bellow might, the
poor, the tenderest, suffer with all their
might: follow follow me! she smiles and
drops a tearless hat unto the floor, with
which she holds on to her skirts.

Pity me pity me, she smiles and writes
away candidacies to inevitable bored fright:
her sense of distances.

Faro

be kind be kind be kind I hear this phrase
screaming in my ear each day, be sweet
be sweet be sweet be sweet this is all
I can say (or seem to say). Alas the phrase the
flare the open door the glare the blare the fan
the flight the high tower reaching up towards glaze
are all I am fit to say, to see to hear to feel
to sway. And the open door fitted into a present
day, most say most say most say most die
on this cross.

The watch-tower, the barrel-hill, the lights go
out, upon the swaying of the hill. It's a plague!
and all bemoan the day the clay the meat
on your fingers.

So that's what they're for, the lighthouse watching
anxiously.

the floss on the mill, she thinks she can read his
will, regardlessly, and terrify those terrible
scarecrows, they're her eyes. Though peering
at his sight, it is impossible that you really meant
it!

Or else sacrifice to those benefices which round
point endlessly to such things as march, read, cough
take your time. In your hands really, since marching
seems to make you go crazy.

Nevertheless there is a point to the story: it ends
at its will's power, circumflexed – strengthened
by arbitration of the will, and a cuckold for all
good will.

Oh, you sweet heart, oh you condescending
minstrel of my tuberculous heart oh the
belly-ache testifying to my withdrawal in
the field of war. Oh the horrors which can not
bring other filth into my nestled heart not
melting in its couch, but the plastic cover
supervising all sing-song. Oh death of
war: oh heart of steel oh the elements withdrawing
from racket.

Oh since you left you wept and felt this
strong tie terminating in exercise of pen
needless to say it was with a hen that he
identified the self – the pen rusting in its
rustic balloon, oval-shaped.

You shaped my heart: it took on a tinge of bartering
softnesses and the tenderness never really died
down. It never really did pry on as it had
previously to the marriage in the kitchen.

I fortunately forget
my sins

It's all humbug: your staring in the face that grey hound: death. It may never be that you do actually meet him, he may come upon you unawares, tenderly you disattentive force him to rely upon your nature.

He lies within your deepest bowels in semi-wrought incandescence. He confirms you as the standing power on the earth: he relies even on your being his propriety. Yet a jowl hangs loose: it is his grasping unawares of your life, as it depends mostly on his male regard for life.

Hit him out judiciously: stand him up for election: there's no grain will not find its streak in his loose house.

softnesses in your belly which will
not come out; irrealisation of your
self which will not shoot out, whence
we cannot decide but in everlasting
strength decide: do your best in the
cannon aroaring.

Distant calls to patriots: severe understandings
petrified hints, and silent disorder
whence we call out help! and fall drit
into a mire which is our belonging.

Steady yourself and gather help from
friends whose double tongue holds fast
even iniquity even the rest from chance's
turning on the wheel.

Hold fast your hands, join them together
if not in prayer then tie them fast
to the chair collapsing vainly in the
rear.

And tie your self to this chair balanced
on its poised ugly legs; tie them fast
hold them together: crackling in the
dust filling your nostrils.

From thence shoot out arrows which
counting on chance unbalance God's
pronouncement: he made you fast! he
made you ring a bell which in all good
cause swung dumb.

No answer? No demise? no wonder you're
not here, not there: he made you fill
your pockets with crumbs, then make
a cake: helpless, bitten into by red
nosed swamps, mice, men, filigrees
turnpikes, swamps again, all trees
bearing down with massive weight. You
have no love affair? with which to
thin our chance's weight? you have
no soul, no God, no love, no help no
stringing in the bushes? Then hold out
your hands, to wipe them clean, of
frog-bits, tyrannies, and withheld simplicities
nestling somewhere in your heart melting
again to fight for a good cause.

And this good cause appeared again
tingling in the shop woods; hitting
out bats, ringing or wringing hearts
out, solacing your husband or lover
marking the time with your fist.

He never let you have your chance's
chance he never let you out alone in
the woods, he never let you despair
at all but that you fought to come
back to the woods.

And here you be: steadying this firm
will with puny silvery embassies, delicate
or delicately wrought crepances, all
the world's fist brought into your
chamber.

Would you shoot it back into the world?
Would you encourage it to kill you?
Would you smile and say thanks? He
will with his slate wipe you clean
of desire's desire, matter's matter
and brotherhood's snare.

And are you crazy really? and are you your
friend's friend? And are you gone quite crazy
sitting and smirking? Enough of beer, we'll
have more clear-cut understanding: this prick
into my shoe will do quite well: it severs
harm from understanding.

And are you then quite well? And have you
called on your neighbors' visions? And are
you gone round the pot fence? quite clear,
quite clear, of misunderstanding?

It is this night we shall see the sun stand
firm in its shoes and winking portentously
to midnight's brooms, lessons, still-lives
and peasants. It is this night we shall see
God's wink: a hold into the round world's
marvelous substance.

Black net stockings: very aware of themselves
and the naked ankle. This is my will: my harshness
my belly's harm: my failure: my hardness, mustering
strength improvised.

This is my belly's harm: my wax, my cry, into
a night filled with authors.

And they cry out pedantically, "we're here
we're our cousin's cousin; we're misanthropy
itself, we're cause and effect truly, nevertheless
why does life swim on?".

Life swims on decidedly restless yet potting
cream unto our backs.

And are you ready now for experience?
Are you willing to face the fight? Can
you admit you hit out badly, carrying
the fire into the heart, the waste and
the corruption?

I have no answer to this corruption. I
cannot place my fist with a two-lighted
lantern in it, into its jam. I am just
jarred into a standstill, with violet
leaves withering about me.

I am no violet lover, I am no scared
crow: I am very near death, its soft
embrace. I have no keys about me, my
heart is of such soft stuff that it cannot
rap out tunes or sing out championships
or qualify a quarrel.

I am not my heart's champion, I am his
guide and fall – its misery never wears
off, but that you cry and fall.

Why do you hamper me with words? why
write this shy story, when all the heavens
on earth are settled on my landlady's
head? Why write words, why shiver so
constantly at this strange point which
is my fellowship with poor haggard men
hugely denied the entrance to wealth
and comfort? I am he that thinks too
much, and my wordings are severed from
this your human bondage – or are they
not, roaming the field in search of this
high blessing?

Beset with fear he hangs to men whose
hollow frockings seem to sneer: you are
divisioned from humankind, you are once
again up on the tree tops, you who would
have shared your soul's handicaps with
all their earth laid bare.

A short walk: you return free: the poorer
men, the savages, they set you free, from
all that greed may overbear.

I am a milk-lady, bringing interesting
supply of food to my brethren, but why oh
why will they not return the fare?

You headstrong sharp end of the mettle behaves
as if, you'd never known harpoons are paid
for wishes, and a cloaked hood haunts your
fare.

Oh why oh why then let my soul (if its existence
sharpens again) have this its fling, when the
valley is gone quite bare? A hundred tunnels
bring you to a quiet place, which is the layout

returning its flare.

A mind quite narrow yet
exhalted: a mind transmitting
its morse code brutally
on chairs painted white.
A mind tapping out the
message you'll not want
to read, pleasing yourself
with my confusion. Yet
it's a telegram! to make
you sigh, or verify me
or explode into rapture.

A mind that does not know
its code, yet in shallow
waters so cold braces up
against the mortified soul.
You may hear its squinting
its tearing the map with
large fat hands, or withdrawing
to diversified code. Its
code! Its tail: its mush
grey matter, and the needle
thrust, fattening the air.

Has it a balance? Has it
a balanced view? Has it
hands and feet, watering
the air? No, its raptures
are too short for comment
and withdraw into caverns
larger than your mouths
when you start speak.

I am no mind – I am a brain
made fast to cajolery, its
breath interlocked with
separate time. No brain
no time – no stinging smile;
a grey lump, an electric
swerve   then all is gone.
Mind sever me from matter
do not lose time, lose it
if you must on despair's
hills, but mock me not!

Quite quiet the breath
takes time: its cajolery
is fast hung to your silent
mind of the matter.

Are you not great? Would you not study?
Then bid the fair its stay; you shall swing
on till daylight, over your books... to
say this night's too long, we've broken
our backs a-flirting.

Will you hang back? Or stay with me? Then
broken-backed men are soft banners to be
hung in the morning, for this year's rest.
Will you sit merrily? And join in the soup?
Then this year's rests, pauses, misshapes
and returning oblong obolos let you perhaps
rest; yet this turn is mine, the next 'tis
yours: and misshapen life hangs on: why,
with the cry on the child's lips?

Because we saw with our mind's eye that
frozen earth no good could give we gave
the ghost its try?

You would not take responsability: you would not
wipe the hinge clean, you would not be a body
rocking through life, or slenderly rapping out
withering tunes. You would be a body, meddling
with traps, and sorrows overshadowing your
own traps.

You would be a body tenderly terrifying the
mice, and your soft heart is stuck through
sunk quietly.

You would sink quietly, ring bells with beards
and beard mice through to not-shadow,
not-willingness, to testify that you were
born.

Would you have me fry in my soup? Or
be the everlasting damsel in her skirts?
Or shove mysteries unto your gaping nostrils
till they were aflame? Or doubt that
ever you were born? Or symposize the
rough rush into your surveillance in
your eyes? Or slander the bellies of
weapons? Then lie still, or down, or
up the roots of this my street: its black
overhangings, my mysteries, swinging
abroad in terrified preoccupation.

I had meant stir the soup on, and it
befell me to stamp my feet on sodden
earth, its tumified vapours.

Accidents befell her and ringingly she
surprised herself saying: "brush the
belt on: it squeezes too tight, and rounds
a belly too thirsty for languor. Yes
I am the mermaid a-vapoured softly into
the night's silvery change, lying on
your swollen palm". Yes, we are in our
tree beckoning to parcels swung out with
careless hands, till we fall.

Till we fall grasping our sides in paradoxical
pleasantry, our onions, their broad swerve
into the nostrils: our onions, and their
smelling the dung out.

Yet on the parcel was written: "shake
me not: let the earth round bare the
point of hopelessness, till we stare
in such a blank fog that never would
one dare say amen, yes, the dog has it,
he has swerved round the point layed
pointedly on the square perturbing this
my round body, its belly-fare".

Onions perceiving the rust in the marrow
or completing the notices or bibliographical
errors on my page. Onions scratching
out the eyes, the places on my skin, the
participation to Parnithopy.

Yes, he has rounded the point laying
squares so blank on the round surface
that seven cats a-browsing could not
lay bare your onions. Yes, he has swung
so far from your good cause that he has
not even the strength to notice that
you were there, at all, in the misery
participating to ours. In the mystery
participating to yours, their good cause
layed flat and burst. Layed square and
present in my wrestle with the devils
small onions rounding the square and
its evil, the belly-boats in your fashion
the hills in your fashion, the fashionable
crowd in the rear-end of meeting places.
Yes he has rounded the square hills which
bellowing my messages tell you be aware
we are you.

We are three, in bush-berries, their
fermentation, in the rear, polished with
bright wax. We are there, punishing your
ransom, and we are there when you decided
it never could come to a final stop.

The stop: the glare the blare the hare
the hinges and the ruts all were there
singing or crying or fornicating or swinging
to a merry tune: your nostalgia, your
unhampered care: my business and your
solace.

*Poems Omitted from the
1992 Edition of* Sleep

I think what we lack is a blue bird leading the way

how many times have we felt the spring on our faces in how many different places.

we shall our better half one day recognize to be our
true god, o would that spring
come!

                              not all
can find their dream
long the road.

o the tangle of inadequacy
rasps cruel into my lombard brain
cutaneously. Sip we the wine.

would it were death i could find all my very soul bursting
aflame, and the wind yelling into my bursting ears with its
sardonic flame. O the road brings out all lust but i sit and
⌈wait for
death's fine flame lest i be eaten by the very life which so
appealingly does call out, lend out its hand
sardonic. In its excitement flame
cannot help its own self out save that i lend it my heavy
⌈hammer
to smother it into deep sick ashes, nor do i dare to smother it
into sick life lest life die out with my very intervention.
⌈So is it i shall
run into the street and wipe the slate clean of all desire or
⌈wait for
the lust to run
its own self out.

well well so we are kissing again the brute's death
at the beaten door. Kill us once and for all
we cry, and you shall see us fly up candid
to clearer moons, to vapourous fumes.

Paul was in his socket all day long and
longed for Divinity, for she was getting
socket-thin and the lust for fever was
an ever tempting thing.

God whoever thou art show thy will, said
the cry-man as he whirled his wings. Whoever
bloats on the other side of heaven is an
angel, said the king of the lust-few. Few
are the men willing to negate our traveller's
science, four fathom deep in the general
waste of the world-wise philosofy. Dare thee
not trust a trial? We will have thee hanged
on the tree of lust covered with the boughs
of the bloated crowd in the heavens. And
the heavens responded not.

Long live the Queen, administered by a few
bloated parishoners. She is a-queening again,
said the Jew in his pillared sand-armour.

Again the road to heaven is not in the
delicacies of the spirit, but in our bodies'
firm will, announced pussy-cat, bloated
with pride of prejudice.

Seven cats went a-queening and saw the remains of the King as he sat a-kinging merrily on old merry england's old armchair. Delay the armoury of thy pronouncement, lest I again make sense!

Firm as was the will of pussy-cat, she
hallowed back to her sphere of action,
less action itself betray a fit of pantomime!
O dearest of friends, thy will to negate
me has harrowed my bones to the core of
their soul-less curve of action fit for
travelling daily but not to love thee as
was preannounced by the King as he sat
on the throne beheaded by the Queen in
a fit of jealousy.

Time a-drivelled in, shocked by the sudden
outburst of several fires in the neighborhood.
Chants of plain company foretold some kind
of disaster, avoided by the merry pitch
of a full glass of wine served by the gallant
waiter. My dreadful pallor brought me to
the full end stop of the road, turned white
with dingy tears. I avoid a full-time stop!
I sing of Christianity! You sing of the
blessed that are so few, yet another chant
portrays your heart... The love which so
few believe possible was in fact impossible.
Woe to the donor of the blood that surges!
He surged wicked by the wicker table, a-syringed
by mechanical practice. Love on the doorstep
waited a-while, then left, pale of a mortal
pallor which never flew off the rose
of Christianity, Christ's blood bathed
in water. Water of mankind agonises near
the table stuck on the edge of the roof
that drops sure of its end. The end thereof
is the martyr of Christ, wicked wicker-chair!
Away on a new battle she fell down her seat
of love and went eat. The smart waiter tenderly
brought out plates and plates of covetous
meats arrayed for her splendour.

If the agents of the universe could watch
coldly the hibernating coldness of our hearts
or contacts as you please they're called,
these rocketing meetings at the eating table
when, when the cold has too deeply set into
the heart, we draw our hearts out through
the eyes which pointedly fix the image we
can no longer retain of friendship or even
love, then there is a chasm, in all due
intercourse, for we cannot see, in our dire
travail, that human bondage has no springs
behind its rasping hold.

Could we see better the light that shifts
unperceived in their marrows, the eyes tranquil
behind the gauze of intentions, whatever
intentions had our hearts, they are wiped
from the table. And with that shift of plans
our heart or gaze surges again unknown towards
a better destiny: to overcome the blank
which nevertheless does prevail, in all
intercourse a plank, leading from your light
to mine.

As if a miser in his treasure hunt, a gun
or revolver pointed at the breast, a simple
trick of feathering the hat, the heart again
unbalances its position afraid it might
blur the grasp. And in the everlasting night
of that afternoon which dragged into a rich
supper we cast our eyes about, devouring
the carelessness of companionship as if
it were our comrade's soul.

This soul which rich decides and bends, two
very uncanny precipices, into our hearts
a jab at nothing then we say: close the
closet that I may better fulfill my or your
purpose – only thing that counts. The only
thing that counts is a bill at the table,
all terminating which sets free – and your
laughter an insult to my mind's eyes or
jabs, the knife drawn at times into your
heart which severely does project its shaft
of dust and light, into my bones.

a disattentive eye, writing all things down
as if a laboratory were this mind, used to
other influences. A pardon for my trilling
eye, which grants, to all labourers, extra
supply of fuel – this night we must die, or
laugh or freeze in the winter grip which
it behoves us to accept.

and the eye in its grain wept, of such inconsiderate
weighing down of matter, melting it down
to fit the matter, restless in its promiscuity
and slandering the pale witchcraft or shaft
of life enstored.

Help! I cannot see your light, I cannot see you
bearing bravely with your might, your fight, your
fist into the matter. Help! You might with every
bright furniture of your soul screech off to
your starting point, and at a roundabout turn,
call for me! If it not were, that you heavily disidentify
your living from mine, which as a mine does roll
around its birth effort.

Help: try me again and find the blaze which so
pronouncedly does spit at its blare: find the
nurse who cares for her patient, till he dies
and leaves her bare. I am no friend of yours
if you but puff and blare at me: I am no friend
of others who turn their gauze on me, levelling
the misunderstanding with a smile. Do turn your
wrongs to this other side of the body, sifting
mildew from the raw bones. Sit and bear your
share of our understatements: till I leave you
bare and broken-necked, a silver fish on the
wood table.

And our misunderstandings did gauze the matter
out subterraneously: they kept us out of the
lavatory of repressed desire and made us fit
for all desire: a cat, a birth right, and a parody
of the best kings.

Whose minds did not so much desire that they
did not see the use for being fit kings: a revolution
in the heart was no matter, if you had your mind
on things.

Which usurped our power; and let loose, even
in minds of kings, jocular composedness, or some
same kind of distress, without a word being made.
Old guests at the table, all wrongs which want
misdoing, and a turn at the gong, or the bottle
and your purchase will be made: let loose all
kings, their minds too jocular do move me to
be a better princess, now that you maroon all
heart into the spirit of the matter.

Vainly we apostrophize, till all shutters
shut, upon our selves, who have forgot
what it is like to be forgot, in so
needy an atmosphere. Vainly we apostrophize
till all drawers shut close and steals
out a worthless sock. 'Tis not our word
which make them so: but our worldliness
which overpowers them.

And in being overpowered there sips
out a tangent smell: old worldliness
caught a-frantic, till it stop.

Till it stop gathering primroses in
the garden of fame: till it stop shivering
with delight at any old stock, fuss,
intermittent cheques, severe misdemeanor
or simple parchment of the tongue. Nevertheless
it rings out bells to its new stock:
stop your bell up and we'll all stop:
till the next paradise, come a-visit
us charmingly, in the long locks of
intermittent friendliness. This shape
which hacks all bodified vices, seems
to say, put off, in candid verse, all
we had to say, lest it be late, to rejoin
old friends, fluttering down the gate.

All friends, in shapes of bells, clinging
to the ear, in an intermittent freeze
which galls us into smiles and reaches
down to our smiles. All friends which
call our authorship: pastime for bedridden
babies, who sit and pout at new birth.

And gall at new birth: simpering verse
which does not quite know how to make
its ends meet. Meeting at that frozen
point where no birth was too late, where
no flower was trampled upon, or spit
at, from the distant land of no one
no authorship, no love for fun in
the red relapse of old things, pattering
to come down the pane.

In transient light mixing the drugs,
got into shape by such fierce withdrawal
as was thought best by the author.
Pattering down to revive the old fire
which had hung shut, in its dark prison
of praiseless blame. Pattering down
panes of windows long since run into
scratches on our minds, small moves,
imperceptible attitudes – long selfish
desire to do more. Pattering down the
rain holds hard our hands, lest we
should forget, its bellows. And screeches
midnight airs, that we may hold a tune
long-lastingly, in our minds beset
with prose. A rugged shape lifting
veils in the enclosure, letting you
breathe air into the rarified lungs,
setting you a-rest in your own boudoir
as if a book holding, leafing, jokingly
letting your head hang galantly.

In a vain stock of praises to forget
that you were born to sound out bells
ringingly into new state: your life,
before it withdrew (together with the
book) into silence. A silence so clearly
put that it shoves out all other fear

of white space, a life so magically
interwoven that it is irrepeatable
though darning at your new sock you
seem to hold it furtherless.

Furthermore adding to the chance that
it may come be stolen on wintry afternoons
and let loose among sheep, parsons,
new drugs, headaches. Furthermore thinking
you will never set it loose, from all
encumbrance, disobedience, transiency
or research. Furthermore obeying the
cricket in the head, who complains
being without parasol. Furthermore
enjoying all this earth's riches, frugality
stopping its flow. And nevertheless
darning your sock, by a fake kitchen
fire, as if all your stock had stopped
breathing, this wintry afternoon, till
you die.

And in dying evolves a strange new
rich scent: your desire, that all such
things should flow, bare upon your neck
till one last square glance at the world
beset you with work, to save that world
which being your own needs mending.
A-mending in the kitchen, under pale
rays of fog, and simply stating you
would prefer not to die. Till all breath
melt, into the shadow of your thought.
Which nevertheless being wrought by
passion, sifts down heavily, at your
morning task, if you wish it to bake
gently. Till in the interwoven woe
rises the douche of new compromise:
a hold on life, a gentle stir from

its encumbrant stiches, weights, marrows
all fit for kings but not for your
prayer which transient assigns your
place to your lot.

Which forever rising and decaying indicates
the soft waves the moon must have felt
on her face, before the sun rose or
shone, on its life-beat, in a stingy
pearl of long shadows, surveying your
little beach, on the side, with all
the oars aside, ready not to make a
run for it, but to stand beside, quiet
as the field-mouse, galloping towards
its hut. Which weather-beaten proved
to be a hole, large enough for a decaying
corpse, large enough for your need,
large in all cases before you rise.
Risen to the skies you meet your friends
and they no longer belittle you but
make wise with the fool. In an exchange
of glances to make wise even the worthiest
of fools – this sing-song dance which
proclaims no dance at all, but wails
its own incompetency out. Out in the
skies to turmoil liftingly with clouds
bent on your saving.

And safe we were, a-frozen in new friendships
uncanny in their precision, while wails
the wind its giant size, unfurled by
the breast, the trees sweeping, the
rails crashing below you.

Who conditioned by life must now stop
look at the incandescence of skies
as if they were your unique abode, now

that life simpering down the valley
slips by unaware. And risks the deflagration
of thoughts which to no purpose now
must bring sense into this new life
since its message is crystal-clear:
a life a-winged, out clear against
a morning olty, which will not dimple
at your fears. Which inexistent flutter
on, a-breast of wings, departing from
midsummer sorrow. Which in all eventuality
fall back upon the heads of those you
left, entrusted with their tales, thoughtless
of your new truancy flipping wide and
loose above their heads, in prayer met.

harsh words follow because he
has none to follow, harsh words
become his mind, a trough in the
dark, an empire of predestination
in his nation. Harsh words follow
shocked into birth, outgiving
verbal opinions of unnecessary
kind – a loud blast of anger.
Words follow, giving his opinion
that no land be wasted. Loud follow
to this his exclamations, vampire
to land, a small cat bought for
nothing.

A burst of gratitude instead
the varied reposes, reactions,
reflections that occur, to his
words, so out of place yet hanging
tight on the boughs. Loud reactions
only to whispers, fringes for
soliloquy. And yet urges, a different
place, high in the nest, where
words may rest. A silence forthwith
came upon her, stole upon her,
her gown of varied tints, and
shone a very riviera of solitude
on its shined breast. Of a blue
kind, quite light, fluttering
if not of gauze – long skirts
not quite trailing in the dust
as they repose, the eye that
figured them. Small diamonds
(false) encrusting them, shining
benevolently at your latin phrase

which turns into horror the very
beetles which grasp at it.

And it shone very proud of its
calm tide, inscribing upon the
dust a quiet tide, of words,
thoughts, opinions, fantasies
too great to bear alone: they flutter
with the skirt when you speak
loud.

And evergreen the boughs bend
back to its passage, an arrow
in the back. Placed smilingly
just a step from power, but not
quite grasping it, nor wanting
to now that it hangs with the
wind.

If my mind were fit a king's, it would survey
all matters of the matter in a grey cloak, from
which poked no transparency, to toddle it off
to the infant's room, a roaring. If my mind were
fit a child's, it would brag about duties. Or
if it saw all round but smiles, it would twinge
with satisfaction, of a round kind, that jokes
at its vanity. But my mind is no fit king: it
pardons, yes, its incumbencies, but tilts toward
leprosy, its black manners, and urgent red desires
a-winged on the slopes. When my mind becomes a
king's, i shift the air from beneath my body, and
cry hurrah, you've done it – but for a short while
larceny against prudence. But now my mind is serf
low geared, low headed and betrayed, by all the
whips which mankind brings to bear, on its slow
back. And sits and chants its prayers, holy on
the tied off bonnet, a-ringing with pleasurable
ears, quite deaf to all honest toil. It cries
you shall help me! and cries on unaware, it had
such tears at its dependence, but for want of
the tear gas most people shove into its premises.

My mind sips on, quite unaware, it may bring on
yet one day on a masterpiece, to fetter all wits
and sing a song of dependence upon its body as
if its strength did not surpass in fact its body's.
Thus chants on hope, a-layed by fear, in a mud
pond, resting from daylight. It were so kind
to imprint upon it some matter, manner to wake
it! But it sits on wailing, its miraculous gears
shall not sift on.

And risking against all privacy a fact quite bare
it waits and waits, some shadows may unbear, its
crushing weight, a wink at darkness, while light
pervades it sinfully, hopefully, crusading against
all borne wishes. It plans no feasts, but would
have danger against it, that it might react with
might, with strength, and crush its opponent's
hair, in a dire chastity of welcome, toddling
it off to the nearest market. It sits on hairs
and bends its way on backwards, juggling with
words, which do not know the sense, and lays even
traps to the evening sourness, which befalls it
if it march on too straight toward want, ambition
all sorts of cants, indecisions, traps, a-wailing
on the turnpikes below its windows, open in the
fear of light, day, consciousness, desire to do
more than it can ever permit rumbunctiously to
care for.

Creative bursts: they do come upon it finally, as
a sing-song in the parley-room, and obscure it
with untried reason, long speeches, and bare feet
upon the carpet, which raising its hairs listens
to the discourse, and pays no care at all, while
it chants on, of purgatory and tried-out medicines
so small you cannot fidget them. And finally it
finds its span: a motive too trustworthy for it
to lay it out in prose, relay it on to mankind
save but in wincing verse, a-ghasted it may fail.

A bird aloft brings on the news, both to its planetary
soul, and to the populace, that it writes on, noble
prose in verse, quite contented, to be later made
a fool of – and it sways on, a-risking fat and
matter current, into the great sweep of its pose
guaranteeing a universal choice, and impediments
to larceny and droves. Yet it chants on, a-mingling

salt tears with precious smiles, on the wings
of aristocracy, yet bending the arrow back, to
make you misfits feel the sense of all companionship.

Which dire in its cell sends out little messages
to all the birds that fly so high towards melting
sorrow, clear prose, and embarking fame. It sends
on messages, as if verse were the minor sister
of queer prose – and still sits wailing! while
it hurts the corners of the table.

I am so much in your power that you do not know
how to keep me, from doing your best now that you
have sworn to lose me. I am so much in your power
that you do not see the key keep the witch. She
trembles on the way to higher affairs, trembles
lest you peer at her, seeing her infusions in the
gaudy night. You do not keep me: you refer to me
thinking I will be calm.

But by destiny she horrifies patrons, peasants,
and her witchcraft, provokes no sound, save that
cry which tense in the night suffers that you be
gone from her apparel, her mind twirling to see
you gone, left off, become a divinized affair,
or a loose branch crackling down.

Peer down my goat of hell, see its juicy
mind gone off at the poignant moment, see
it describe hell's atmosphere with as much
gaud as if it were a summer's day. See it
now turn the bay, wrestle with your image
which pales off – now that you have severed
it.

Do not count on my being obedient – I see
no other way to the upstairs heavens than
that of writing you off: squibbling with
the farmers, and separating you from all
imagery.

Disappointed you will turn the bend, seek
me out one day – tremble lest I have already
forgot your apparel, your mind, your means,
your doubtful behavior – yet the goat counts
three, then leaves, – you dry on the mountain
slope.

Rocks overshadow her – they imprison her
suffering, drying off now piece by piece
she will master your impudence, sit back
and stare.

An idea is a host, embarrassed it might
resign its post. A swift circle is the
might allowed for twelve kidnappings, down
the right side of the post.

On eleven outsets did I resist the making
of fire through the doors of heavens like
this my brain; small fires round a circle
sweeping the strain away.

Yet an evergreen bush denies triumph; you
are not my personal choice but an everlasting
care that I should not fail, disturbing
the face of this earth.

In a race which has no fathoms, since we
provide it with fuel and food, to touch
the evergreen. May he dream who wins the
rally. Yet in shimless apostrophe drives

on the cart to its sunset the sunrise striving
to force you below.

Undefeatable it rested on its lover's arms
unrested but withholding all triumph while
nodded the beast. Slip in manyfold, into
this green jacket which denies not its
folds to the attentive.

Brought out fresh candy, ate it all, and replaced
the parley with cherubs smiling
at each other's faces. Slipped triumphantly
into the roads marked with a dew which
resembled mud but stuck not on the reversible

boots. Life a-swimming ran into a corner
for the contrasting objects to obey it
slowly, or the rest of the battle which
being left to Christ, seemed surpassed.
Yet another hill covers the bosom of the

painter with its scarlet gauntlet: a surmise
that you'd never know the truth about
him.

Hell's shafts are too sudden; I envy parley
which allows rich endowments for humour and
never separates witchcraft from desire. Hell
itself is too sudden, and its ramshackle shafts
are no fit adjectives for my connubial chatters
on the rimless edge of philanthropy.

Hell's shafts are too risky, and endanger
my thinking of every thing a pearl, a damnation
on the swift side of thinking.

I am no host, but the prayer met; in stead of
grants from our stateshood, widowhood in tears
through the blank fog.

Triumphant you swing into a life which
many believe stirring. Then appropriately
you let loose various criticisms. Notwithstanding
all the road seems covered with mulberry.
Next – a slippery footpath, for all to tread
on, a rose in the morning twilight showing
the way. Which lost rose to the occasion
and rasped out several conjunctions, fit
to appear before the king, as a thing set
by circumstance. Yet no leaf had stirred
while you let out your breath generously
to invite corruption.

Naked on the bough it swung into its scarlet
gaud of stride, striving to appear noble
while it played a part in more than one
murder. It sanctified its mother, abolished
its father, ran loose arms open to its
children, played cricket, ate the grass
sat on the upholstered storage-room. With
a look on its eye to drag you from suffering
into a better pit, or an allegory of things
too old to be past. Yet no writer had ever
perceived it before as it munched blades
with the cut in them for your bastard fingers.
Set with grips it invites all and none
to the ball, too lazy to feign armistice.
And the bells of the town pealed out laughter
in so dizzy a scheme that it fell apart
right on the edge of the lawn. Where kings
and murderers played the play, lent each
other pennies, or dropped from the game
altogether, to blush for shame. State
not your meaning – the game is plain – the

wreck is in your mother's tits. And bit
by bit she rolled on, feigned, grew an
allowance, perceived the dew on the other
side of the ministry, but plunged into
the world's rack with such gaud (unperceived
by its mother) that no end of the game
could satisfy her bulging cramps in the
stomach. Stomached all, withdrew into its
fake ministry, bade all goodbye, till
the next wave of jewels might don her hands.

And they forgave her; the common sin was
to all a mercy – rambling on necessarily
to plant the plants in the garden. A fake
square, or a crusade, rectangular in shape
common property to feeding hands, and mishapen
gaud to all propriety a fitting minstrelship
led on the race. Which paltry could not
stop short of breath, lest it crumble with
the sight of the sea, and the rising air.
The sun obliquely retired into its chambers
was not there at all when she swung again
into shape. Sunless, moonless, the race
ran on – the vapid horizon could not be
seen, as the mist covered all property
with glances of an indifferent sort, to
so much common forsaking. No battleships
no stakes, no bets, no plaids in the victory
only the red conscience forebearing, the
sun setting too low, and the minstrel awaking
to its fate, its late understanding. Setting
the pace, forgiving the brave, upholding
the petty too brave to bear the weight, she
slipped into the canvas tent, slid her
arm into its joint, drew out knives with
pointed pens, and told all, still simpering
with the joy of participation. There sits

your story: it never had tale-bearers, never could stand on its feet but that you have nudged it into being.

He isn't ready for a balanced approval of this
year's new register. He lives on a dream and
separates marshes from ends. He is imprisoned
by his own inconstancy. He dreams, yes he dreams
that he will marshall the field, but the mud
crackling at his boots shivers when seeing his
eyes. He is notwithstanding all an element of
impartiality, a return ticket to slender boots
of gain, the power in them.

I am not his sister, but tend to lance three-
fold embraces into the air, at his shivering.
I am not his banker, but want to learn a new
way to forge his constancy, into my arms dewed
with navel. I am not his belonging but want
to insist on his leaving me. He and I are the
two-fold union of breaths. Without circumstance
is there no denial; without his breath is there
no hating it.

In a red room close to the fire is the row of
his books, heavy-learned, in rows of challenging
usurpation. In the room the light bends triangularly
into his thick forehead; in his room i bend
a back towards melting. No meeting – no soup
for the invited prince, or the sister, or its
contrary – a shallow vessel. The plate low-standing
belongs to the crude marshes of the world and
its jacket lined with frost or candy for children
with bitten lips, sparkles into darkness, if
the row and the list and the child and the room
and the prince and the woman carry out their
song. Which will not descend toward better bet
in life than their own inconsistency.

Serene sets lay off the bet but for the hour gonging; no abrupt end to marshes: I am his sister in the navel, he is my prince in the heart, you are his king in the juice; I am his row of dominion.

Why do you want to dream? Why cry, why recite
this year's prayers partaking of vivacity
in the world a-resting? Why disengage your
self from upheavals penetrating into your
sound blood? This year's tiger sings he crashes
into this year's arms.

And this year's lovely widowhood sings it rests
in three arms: Noè, the singer and the bird
nestling frank into the arms of a bush-berry
partaking of this year's merriness.

Please sing! please nod your head gravely
or graceless; intending I should marry.
Think about it, purse your lips, partake of
this night's advantages merrily.

And he souped with his soul that night crying
in a wilderness which was not frank but gave
thought to thought, alphabet to words, or
engraved sorrows in a line, comforting your
bedless grace.

And sitting with the birds that cried willingly
to please his God. Who sat watching, all mysteries
from afar, regardless of their soul. Which
turning the round point saw him sitting restlessly
behind their backs, waiting for their arrival
in the juicy period of grace, its listless
charm, its annoyance at being first fed, then
challenged. And rounded the point: and fed
its grace, and withal seemed to rest in his
Grace.

Three-pointed Grace: forgive our sins as we forgive those that sin them.

He cannot rest on his laurels; he must
fight his way back to primitive innocence
as it was conceived by his maker, but
his two way sword swings sharp and off
the true mark, lying on his feet, the
soles touching.

He must rest awhile, then turn back
to screws and ledges, and fetch gangsters
from his soul, rapidly running from
mistakes, which he never committed but
only dreams he did as he is told.

And then he falls, to death despair
(poor words) and sits the chair, extravagantly
rearing its children up, leaning all
the while against a wall, which is his
own mental picture of himself as he
brays gently into cattle herds and peaches
too round for marshes.

He may not die, he may still live and
die, sing true without marshmallows
turning mixing in his blood. Else sing
a song of plain chant, against again
a wall so bare that he may tremble, lest
the chant pierce his heart through.

Beauty is not enough for him: he must
lay bare all faults, till they turn
on a turnpike and strike him bare. Heart!
cannot you decide one way or another
regarding the lack of sing-song in my
plain heart?

He sings quite bare: his hair stands
on end: he will be plain and make shelves
grin at their stupidity. But beware:
thrice, or three times does care come
to turmoil round his legs, arms, blank
ankles – steadying his vision, till he
sit bare: bloodless at last, ready for
the killing – done in a moment, if you
please, while all stand stare.

Do you really think that reality is so unintelligible?
Is it this you mark with the tip of your
nose? Is my feeling for comfort in your
sagacity not a sign of willing the earth
to come round the point? Are you not yourself
a small tyrant, in your blind way, and
are you not my small teacher, prayer, everlasting
free guide? Am i to disobey you to find
earth as round as the square you seem to
fix, pointing at necessity, amusement, relaxation?
To damn my soul is my soul's hope; it will
be born of you: and your blindness lightens
my sundry needs, my bull fight, my remonstrance
your own blind toe; your shoemaker.

He hangs in blind drips from the square
clouds at the hidden horizon; he tips the
necessity, the silence, you seem to need
and fear: he gains, by controlling my body
and your shoe (as it trips) three times
the hopes we want to drive, hang, enchannel
or guide to small events, round shaped earthen
manifold blunted purposes. He is the shaven
headed God: he is man's prime mystery, the
builder of fire, as it constructed your
capitulation.

Three times seven hopes: three bells ringing
the ear, as it in its first firm shape allows
no sound but one: a dribbling monotony, a
sound of fornication: a thrice rising bell
in the hill of your desolation. Rise up
and start, laugh off the crowd: it waits
it bangs even through your armour, now that

with sudden purpose you survey: angels rounding
the bell off, tipping it as a cup into wine
frothing at our lips, which round with
yawning surprise, do as they wish: he wishes:
stand firm aghast: they may never fail.

They fear: they may never come round the
hill of your consolation.

why not slip out of chance's way? give way
to improvised dances? Or promise God (who's
mighty head rolls on) to do as he wishes:
stir the soup on

Why not demise the headlong roll from entirely
new pay rolls, alphabets cringing to a stop
repeating endlessly: thou shalt not stop.

Yet i stop: and pause to think, since heavenly
headlong bright purposes do not seem to think
i shall roll on.

And yet also the house is full of ghosts!
they stir gently, breaking their hearts to
see that the pay roll is not really coming
on.

Woe to me, woe to my donor: he stands reckless
easily stirred by my heart which jumps out
of bartering, visiting, telling old tales
a thousand times more.

stand still and think: till all agony has
me bethink: you are a friend, truly friend
shimmering in the light.

pause now on brink: till all the agony has
poured its slender self down, this hill which
is my belief you think: to hell's care, this

her bright new face, her turnip hands, her
defenceless smile, or her two-lipped smirk

which rows a boat a thousand miles.

An idea is a host, embarassed it might
have to resign its post: a post is a
hot tower, lying in the midst, no, peeking
through high clouds. Your tumble among
the heathen (the heath was white with
thunder), your tumble among the furs and
stripes of creation had you lie still
quietly almost, reading into witches'
hands, down the road of gospel.

Your idea is a host, selling screams for
bewitchery, breaking those clouds through
with triumphant haste, taste of the battle.
i am not without despondency cried he
to the upper story man: i am not without
haste yet cannot remember my name, even
those eleven syllables which formulate
my taut world, those words with which
you announce, enounce, and despair, even
those words, with which you despair heredity
renown and gain, lost in a featherdown
spirited like most, but unobtainable,
emprisoned in this dark closet, my year's
plague.

Had you thought of saying what lay on
your mind you would have scribbled down
divers signs on a scratch of paper: and
tied down to earth with its forged iron
bell, all those pronouns interesting you.

Which bent and pulled, and screamed off
turning the corner in haste. I am not
this year's plague but announce, idiosyncrasies

turmoil in my blood, correctitude and
tantrums in ink, bell-shaped, almost
unpronounceable, till they lie square
athirst for pronunciation. Here lies
A.R. – she sits, lies, stands, drinks
twists her mind out of order then puts
it back again into order, with a thin-
lipped smile, a jaunt on her new face
and a triangular smirk on her fat hips
rounding the point, rounding the point!
of belligerency.

She is set to rest on her graveyard walk
and will regard no one with studious love
now that her walking stick sticks into
the mud, prying straight into a heart
of mud.

you suffer, then are gone, to the back
woods, enhanced by silver mystery,
it hits you back but you stand almost
firm, as in a fairy-book, all stern
are the roses.

And creep into your shell mysteriously
dancing in round shapes, or forgiving
this backwards sperm. Delight is delight
lost tales are lost, late calls are
gone, then it is midnight.

With all your might you stand and sign
silvery bits of paper, till they stand
nigh covered with footprints, blue
prints, or finger's prints, holy on
the house. This house which will no
rot allow, this house which will no
grasp allow, but that it be the kindest
work into the world.

And then decide: we'll have no more of rejuvenated
blood, or water's water: we'll dance no more
on the perked apple-tree, we'll sing no more
love's lesson.

We'll drink a bottle of beer, tear it down
gallantly, and then surmise (since in sleep
he did not appear) that he left, for another
shadow.

I me you the others, swinging a-neck-tied on an
empty entrance; I me you the others swinging to
time; I you me and those poor others, following
afterwards towards a greater glory: I me you the
others singing a-field astrand and unworthy to save
their neckties.

Meaning that I mean that I cannot try to bishop
the field nor house the cat till he rolls by lopping
meaning I am stronger than you are.

Meaning that I am younger than you are. Meaning
I am far less stronger than you are or weaker as
the sun, the wheel turn.

Wheeling through midnight airs the superficies trembling
as we both step crash through them. Bothering to
sift mid-night matter from stubble or stubborn grey
matter a-ringing rusting in the nests offered. Or

hiding again later to melt the sauce down. Unhankered
by afterthought or paradises waking to see you beckon
out of way of harm.

Time can stop either for good
or for bad; it shivers impertinently
with wide hoary mouth, or stops
and cries I've had enough: of
this belligerence.

Time is no belly; it is a harpoon
smiling wisely or popping jokes
while you serve your master broken-
hearted.

Time sews and mends! And inquires
into your swift broken thinking
why have you let the marmelade
go wrong? I am no harpoon cried
the joker, time has no ruts for me
said the fishmonger; all is
all, time is time, swung out
of the heavens.

A pearl, a sacrifice, a singing
report of deaths... I am no joker
cried the fishmonger, my hand
and heads sing that time has
all its shivers marked to time.

Eleven horses went mulberry picking
thinking that they would grow
old but time instead sat and

sewed, regardlessly of their
wide open mouths, their caverns
longing for more.

Eleven races were set going, free
lance thinking yet grew old: time
still sat thinking, he'd never
grow old. Misshapen mishaps, paradises
turnt sour – all are in the horses'
mouths, their terrified bellies.
Time a-thinking squared the hole.
Time a-worried strove to grow
old. Time a-sitting stuck to
his seat: no battle more terrified
than this was in my hold.

I have harpooned time: he sits
mulberry picking stuck to his
seat: yet broken cries slip out
the mouth: time has no shivers
no other place than earth!

Yet we will mark the time he
grew huge enough, carrying barrels
to the waste land, or turning
carrots into turnips, or otherwise
occupying his selfless soul. Time
has no pickings! he may grow
old, if it were not for my pickings
severing the whole.

Turnips ramshackle smiles at
this: are you not prepared for
battle yet? Is your shaft so
light? Cumbersome nature will
return the flight: you will die,

and grow strong, smoking turnpipes
or other wrongs.

Which smoking silver dishes dug
their graves light enough to
carry straight to that heaven
where time has no wrongs, no
ruts to fist with. Yet all the
while your smile does harm, with
a willow-will, carrying the song
a misery interlaced with white
time, softer than my belly's
charm, its doings outdoing you
while you stand strong.

Quite quiet you lay off critizing, anyone but
this high tree, your sovereign. I've turned mystic
it shows in the empty pockets.

O man o man o man without whom there is no mercy
for woman o woman o woman's tense fright: be my
God then or excuse your flight.

His flight? My flight – oversure it's no blight to
race from filanthropies, or races in the delicacies
of the heart, their tear-dropping. You mysterious
man, a-couch me, then come no more: your stinging

sigh is not worth my rebellion. He's gone quite
off you, left you to your proper cloud? Joy then
is the liberty i take with dogs, trains, paupers
or my mind's flight.

Why is my splitting of personality so raw
why is my spelling so mistaken, why is my
publishing so low, why then while waits tender
time embracing why then are you so low. This
this writing is itself is dangerous this this
writing below is for the waist's belly-boat.
I mean that whence we'll fly to paradise with
better bows, arched against time.

Why are my better books so loud, that they
finger the paper turned into them, why does
this my freeze squeeze low and again this
mark below.

Time marks hollowly Hallowe'en: it dances frightfully
'round your shirt. Hence go, hence depart,
hence ply this bow, wheezing into the air
while brave airs chant the merry bough.

I am a singer cried the he-man, wildly
tumbling mid-heath into forgiveness. Are
you the entrance out said she feigning disorder
of the mind and of the brain. No your earth
has too many sharpened points to it said
the rolling keyboard.

We are in the nest travelling through a
barren land which has no face to its presence
while the skies turn purple and out of
order: would you rather revolve around
the moon's substances fixing you in the
face or swear you are my master's daughter.
No – the king is out of shape, he is a-weary
of this night's revel; goodnight to you
the revolver hanging on the side.

Why? because you spoke too long of bravery
and the horses ploughing out their own
deaths, because you spoke too strongly
of this year's new hat, its misery, its
mastery, its penetrating abode in the witchcrafted
attitudes, the soul, my Antigone.

Death staring straight at you in the face
while hums a gentle stir of winds broken
winged hopes.

Twelve Poems from Sleep

Translated by the Author

4

Bene, dunque, pazienza alle nostre anime
i mari scorrono freddi sulle nostre nude gole
tremanti. Mangeremo dalla nostra vuota mano
sorridendo vani. La brocca d'argento s'è chiusa di scatto;
noi scattiamo via dalla noia, in un batter
d'occhio. Tentacoli di passione corrono a mo' di rosa
come fiammeggianti lingue di opaca rossa lava.
                                    [La nostra anima
strappa con passione, il suo caminetto. Il vento grida oof!
e se ne va. Fummo lasciati soli col nostro fratello –
ombelico. Benissimo, così impareremo a
violentarlo. Soli. Parole nella loro fornace.

                                                (1955)

17

oh gli alberi sono scossi di tensione invernale
e le foglie si precipitano su d'un vasto fondo
galloppo-cavallo
(e le foglie ruzzolano come uccelli selvaggi per
                                    [la brughiera)

                                                (1955)

19

oh le scialuppe escono in mare e noi restiamo a riva
masticando il pane salato del
disastro (la sua è una usata
frase, e infatti la
preferiamo).

(1955)

25

no non ti amavo capisco questo chiaramente di nuovo
                  [o io penso che
trovo il mio cuore fondamentalmente freddo ma
era dapprima una calda pietra, supplicando
d'aiutarti a giungere ad un punto ultimo
tra di noi, e così di nuovo mi separo da te e
mai più debbo tentare di farti succube
in mia mano, mai più porrò la
ascia tra di noi mai più a te correrò gridando
vedi questa musica!

(1955)

27

questi pensieri che tanto attraentemente m'avevano
                  [ravvicinato
al tuo essere
debbono essere gettati, ch'io non possa morire.
oh che sia la vita che noi nonostante tutto
allontaniamo, stranamente dolce,
oppure che sia dio che giochi destro con me, che mai più io
t'incontri, al punto ove ogni desiderio
muoia, e la gioia soltanto
governi
le macchine affuocate.

(1956)

un soffice sonetto è tutta la forza che ho
di creare, piena e facile vita ho sempre e per sempre
di nuovo e di nuovo distrutto, ma forse era dio che gridava
in me spegni tutte
le luci! Nessun amore è concesso a colui che
odia ogni amore eccetto la vita
scritta su carta là corre il mio
seme folle alla
morte.

(1956)

ah allora avevate pensato avreste trovato la felicità
al bar all'ang-
olo, e siete ancora una volta delusi, oh voi che aspettate
senza tempo alle fontane e siete respinti nella propria
tana. mai più mai più diciamo ad
ogni separazione dalla
gloria, mai più illuderemo i nostri sensi la nostra stessa
essenza, che di nuovo possa scorrere il sangue fresco sul
[bianco
ceppo. Portate il vostro pesante fardello di erbe secche
[portate
il vostro dolore e tenetevelo stretto raggelato alla vostra
essenza, potrebbe scindersi in
bianca luce, se soltanto vi
scavate.

(1956)

abbiamo di nuovo imparato a peccare, a cantare ciò
è, con l'accetta alle nostre
spalle ma comunque noi

cantiamo
selvaggiamente
prima che dio scopra la nostra disgrazia, presto
nascosta nelle ali di ogni
falsità, la gioia è perennemente
un dolore.

(1956)

32

un centinaio di volte debbo scavalcare gli alberi tigri
che possono scoppiare le melagrane. Oh lebbra
che m'assalisce, il vento canta purpureo
ai miei orecchi pieghi, i mari divengono purpurei
ai miei occhi ciechi, e io canto (io sprofondo) nella
nera preghiera della notte, più morbida di tutti gli alberi
tutti i cieli tutti i mari.

(1956)

34

Molto prima che l'estate si fosse involata, erba verde
marciva al suolo: – molto prima che il mio cuore e
il tuo si fossero esauriti, di nuovo la verde erba iniziò
a germogliare. Molto prima che il metro del nostro amore
trovasse misura, il mio cuore s'era esausto e
il sole ancora brillava fisso e liquido ai miei
occhi stanchi. Molto prima che mai tu avessi giocato con
il caso, il caso t'aveva partorito. Allora diventammo
tutti muti. Molto prima che riposassimo nell'iniquità
il caso aveva recitato la sua parte.

E fu allora che lasciò il convento (l'interminabile
letto da malato). Allora lasciò la carità! Allora trovò
[la speranza.
Allora se n'andò.

(1958)

Index of Titles and First Lines